Children's Atlas
of
The World

Contents

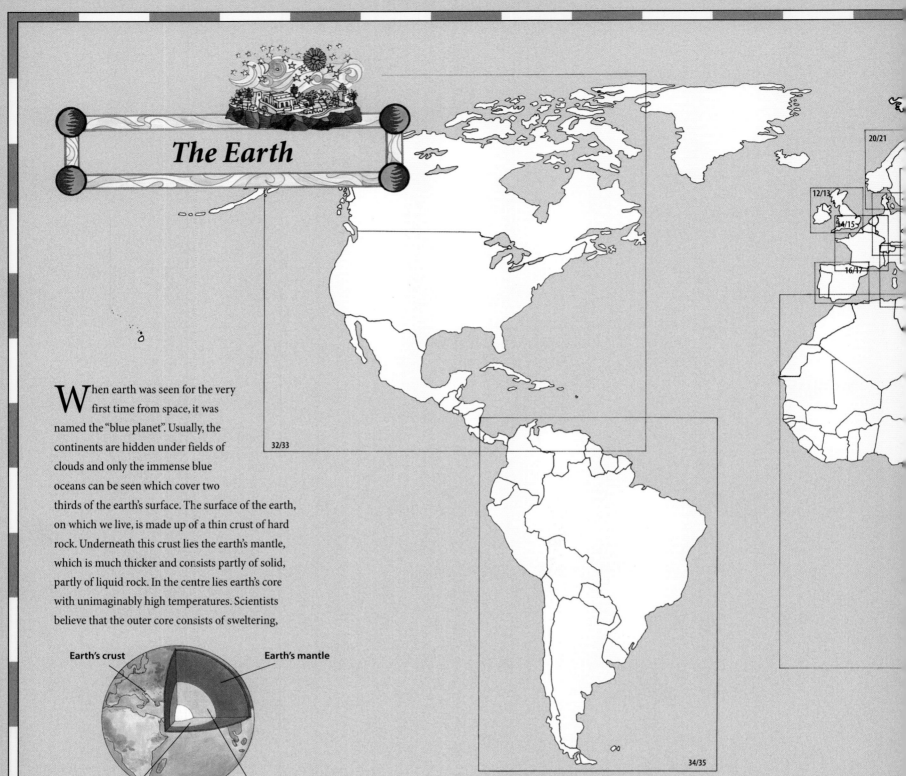

The Earth

W hen earth was seen for the very first time from space, it was named the "blue planet". Usually, the continents are hidden under fields of clouds and only the immense blue oceans can be seen which cover two thirds of the earth's surface. The surface of the earth, on which we live, is made up of a thin crust of hard rock. Underneath this crust lies the earth's mantle, which is much thicker and consists partly of solid, partly of liquid rock. In the centre lies earth's core with unimaginably high temperatures. Scientists believe that the outer core consists of sweltering,

Earth's crust

Earth's mantle

Inner core

Outer core

fluid iron, nickel, and oxygen, while the inner core is made up of a ball of solid iron and nickel.

The earth's crust consists of various independent plates. They swim on top of the liquid rock. At some parts these plates push together, at others they break apart. This is why, in the course of many millions of years, the continents have migrated. Approximately 270 million years ago there was only one continent called Pangaea. At some point, Pangaea broke apart and the continents began to spread over the entire hemisphere. Even today the plates move and by doing so cause earthquakes and volcanic eruptions. The earth has seven continents with many individual

nations. The continents are: North America and South America, Europe, Asia and Africa, Australia and Antarctica. On the above map of the world, there are rectangles that indicate which parts of the earth are highlighted on the following pages.

270 million years ago, there was only one single continent. It is called Pangaea.

In order to facilitate orientation on earth, vertical and horizontal lines were used to divide the planet into sections. The horizontal ones are called latitudes. The medium line, also called the Line, is the Equator. From here, the circles of latitude are measured towards the north and south in degrees.

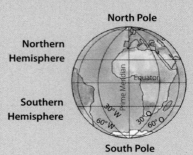

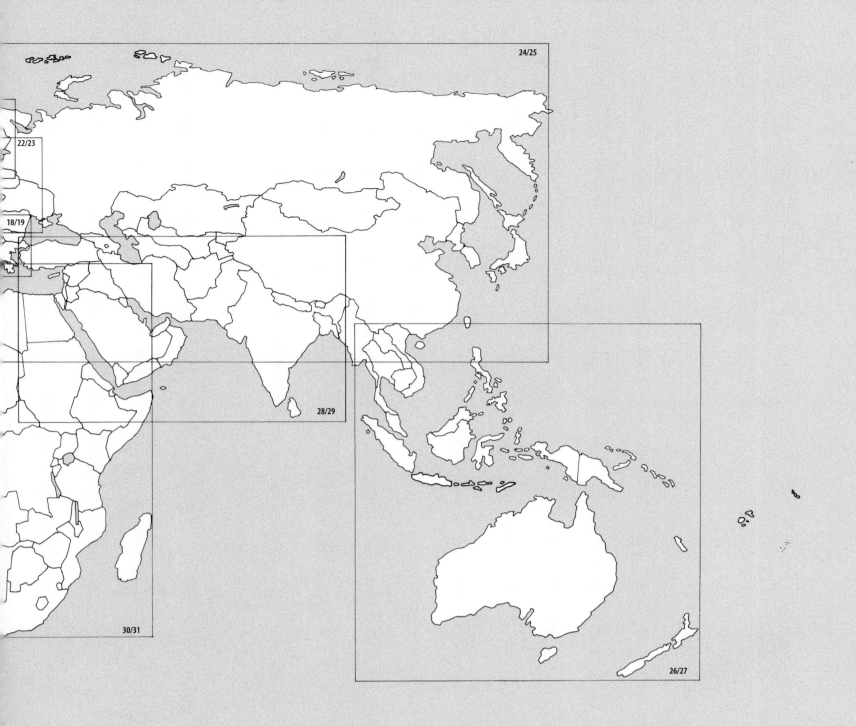

22/23

18/19

28/29

30/31

26/27

The vertical lines are called longitudes or meridians and are measured in degrees towards the east and west, starting from the Prime Meridian, the zero-degree point of longitude, in Greenwich, London. Earth takes 365.25 days to travel around the sun. At the same time, the earth rotates around itself once within 24 hours. This means that the sun never really rises or sets; it is the earth that is turning so that each country has one half of the day under the sun's rays and the other half is spent in darkness. The axis around which the earth rotates is slightly tilted. This is why one half of the earth comes closer to the sun than the other and it explains the seasons: the side inclined towards the sun is warmed up more – we call this summer – whereas on the other half, winter reigns. Since the rays of the sun hit the Equatorial terri- tories nearly in perpendicular fashion, this part of the earth is hottest. Towards the Poles, on the other hand, the temperature decreases. But it's not just the latitude that determines the climate.

In the higher parts of any given country the climate is cooler than in the lowlands. Warm or cold ocean currents can influence the climate just as much as clouds, winds, and vegetation.

It takes one year for earth to travel around the sun.

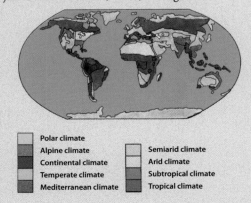

Polar climate	Semiarid climate
Alpine climate	Arid climate
Continental climate	Subtropical climate
Temperate climate	Tropical climate
Mediterranean climate	

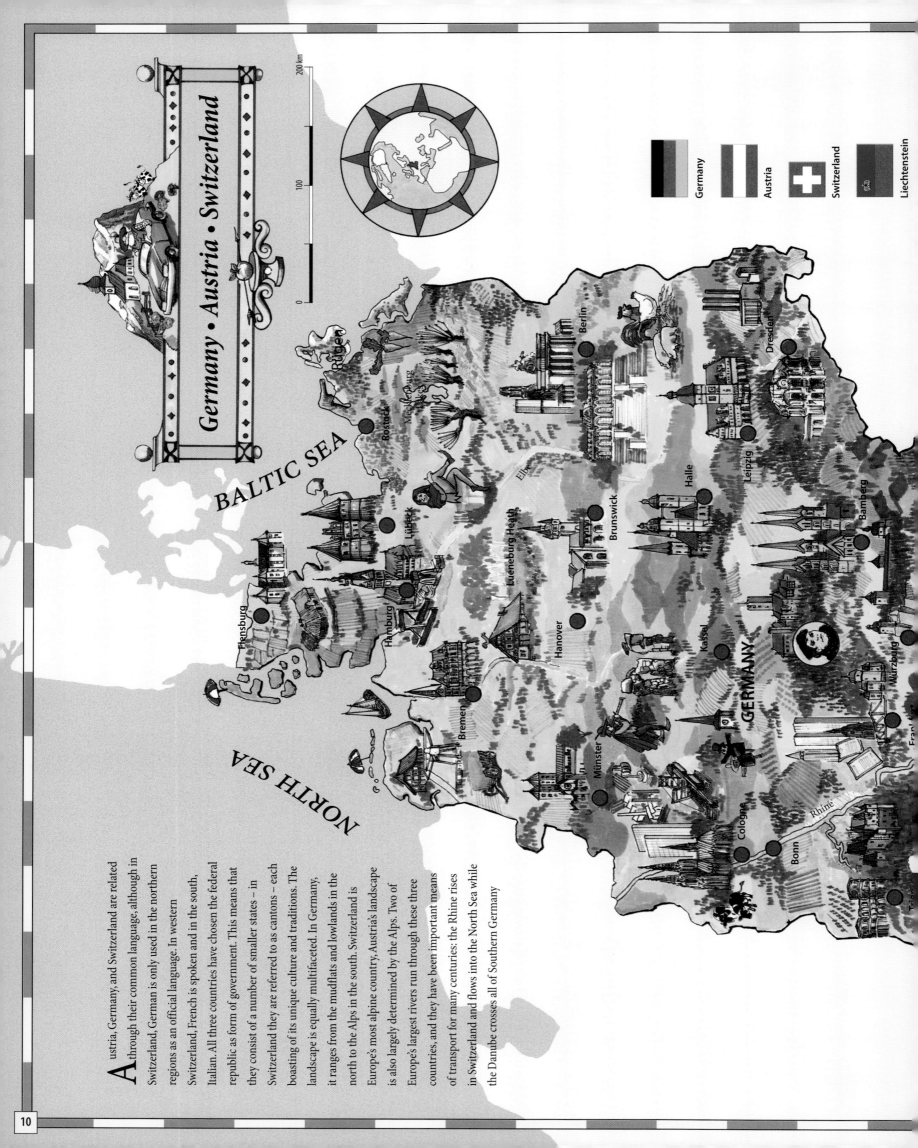

Germany • Austria • Switzerland

200 km

100

0

Germany

Austria

Switzerland

Liechtenstein

BALTIC SEA

NORTH SEA

GERMANY

Rügen

Mecklenburg

Rostock

Berlin

Dresden

Leipzig

Halle

Elbe

Bamberg

Lübeck

Lueneburg Heath

Brunswick

Flensburg

Hamburg

Hanover

Kassel

Würzburg

Bremen

Münster

Frank

Cologne

Rhine

Bonn

Austria, Germany, and Switzerland are related through their common language, although in Switzerland, German is only used in the northern regions as an official language. In western Switzerland, French is spoken and in the south, Italian. All three countries have chosen the federal republic as form of government. This means that they consist of a number of smaller states – in Switzerland they are referred to as cantons – each boasting of its unique culture and traditions. The landscape is equally multifaceted. In Germany, it ranges from the mudflats and lowlands in the north to the Alps in the south. Switzerland is Europe's most alpine country. Austria's landscape is also largely determined by the Alps. Two of Europe's largest rivers run through these three countries, and they have been important means of transport for many centuries: the Rhine rises in Switzerland and flows into the North Sea while the Danube crosses all of Southern Germany

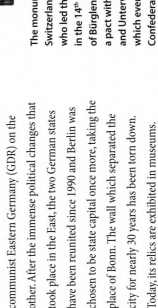

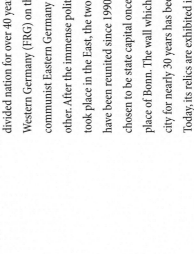

The monument of William Tell in Altdorf, Switzerland commemorates the legendary hero who led the successful Swiss liberation movement in the 14th century. Tell came from the village of Bürglen in the Uri Canton. In 1291 he made a pact with leaders of the Cantons of Schwyz and Unterwalden, referred to as the Ruetli Oath, which eventually led to the formation of the Swiss Confederacy.

and Austria and then leads to the Black Sea far away to the East. The Rhine is navigable from the Swiss town of Basel onwards. This is why many important centres of industry and commerce are based along its banks. In Basel, chemicals are produced. Alongside precision instruments and clocks, these are the most important export goods of Switzerland. Further north along the Rhine, in Ludwigshafen, Cologne, and Leverkusen, are the German centres of chemical industry. Heavy industry is centred in the area of Duisburg, where the world's largest inland port is. Germany exports machines, cars, and aeroplanes throughout the world. In Austria and Switzerland tourism is much more important for the economy. Millions of holiday makers come here every year to go skiing or mountaineering in the Swiss and Austrian Alps; strolling along the magnificent arcades in the Swiss capital Berne or tasting a piece of delicious Sachertorte cake in Austria's capital Vienna. After the Second World War, Germany was a divided nation for over 40 years with democratic Western Germany (FRG) on the one side and communist Eastern Germany (GDR) on the other. After the immense political changes that took place in the East, the two German states have been reunited since 1990 and Berlin was chosen to be state capital once more, taking the place of Bonn. The wall which separated the city for nearly 30 years has been torn down. Today, its relics are exhibited in museums.

Only few people live on the island of Helgoland in the North Sea, but thousands of seagulls, guillemots, and fulmars populate the colourful, red-hued sandstone rocks.

Wolfgang Amadeus Mozart, the ingenious composer and musician, was born in Salzburg in 1756 and died in 1791.

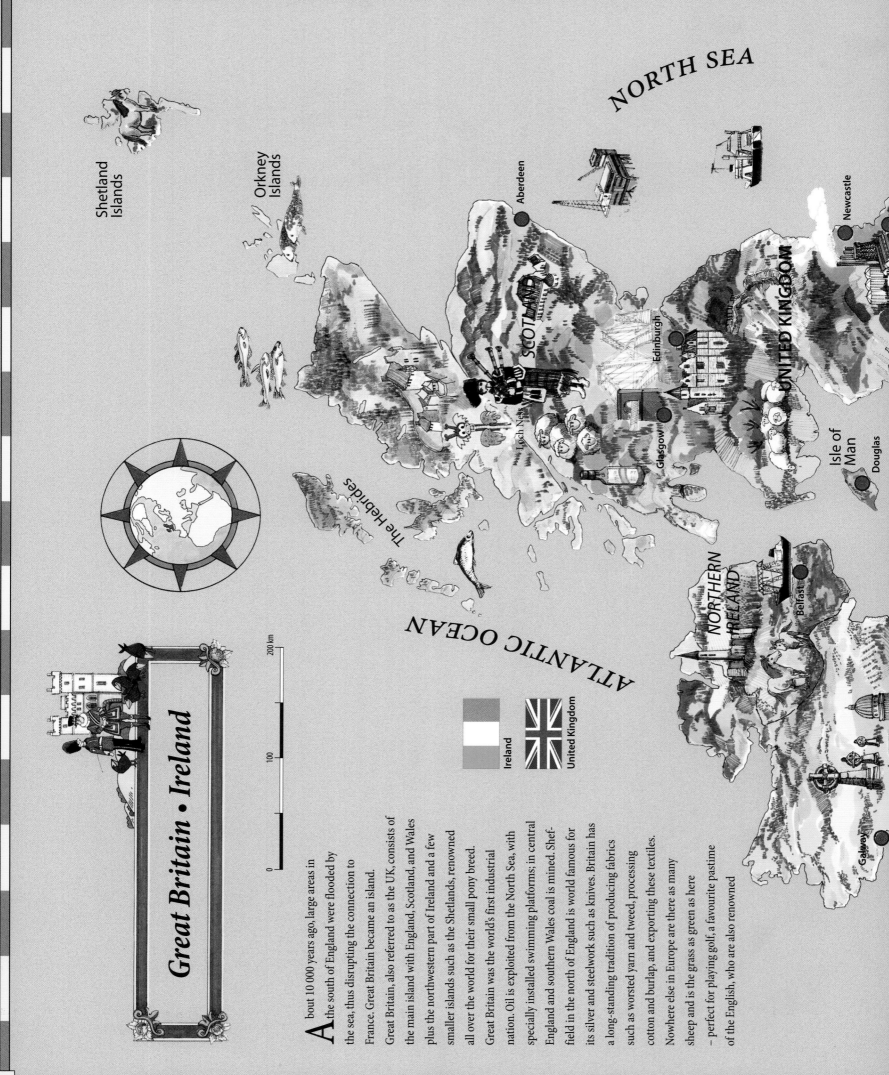

Great Britain • Ireland

About 10 000 years ago, large areas in the south of England were flooded by the sea, thus disrupting the connection to France. Great Britain became an island.

Great Britain, also referred to as the UK, consists of the main island with England, Scotland, and Wales plus the northwestern part of Ireland and a few smaller islands such as the Shetlands, renowned all over the world for their small pony breed. Great Britain was the world's first industrial nation. Oil is exploited from the North Sea, with specially installed swimming platforms; in central England and southern Wales coal is mined. Sheffield in the north of England is world famous for its silver and steelwork such as knives. Britain has a long-standing tradition of producing fabrics such as worsted yarn and tweed, processing cotton and burlap, and exporting these textiles. Nowhere else in Europe are there as many sheep and is the grass as green as here – perfect for playing golf, a favourite pastime of the English, who are also renowned

NORTH SEA

ATLANTIC OCEAN

Shetland Islands

Orkney Islands

The Hebrides

SCOTLAND

Aberdeen

Loch Ness

Edinburgh

Glasgow

UNITED KINGDOM

Isle of Man

Douglas

Newcastle

NORTHERN IRELAND

Belfast

Galway

Ireland

United Kingdom

0   100   200 km

ENGLAND

WALES

IRELAND

Dublin

Cork

Liverpool

Manchester

Nottingham

Birmingham

Cardiff

Bristol

Plymouth

Southampton

Brighton

London

Dover

Trent

Ouse

Thames

Severn

ENGLISH CHANNEL

for enjoying their daily cup of tea.

As a nation that grew through seafaring and trading, the country has many shipyards and large ports, as in London and Liverpool. For centuries, trading vessels would leave Britain and venture out to many far-away countries, setting the logistic and economic basis of the British Empire. London, the busy capital with its famous red busses and black taxicabs, lies on the banks of the river Thames, by its estuary mouth. In the UK, people drive on the left. The Royal Family resides in Buckingham Palace; Parliament and Scotland Yard, famous for its clever inspectors, are also located in London.

The craggy, mountainous north of Britain with its firths and lakes is inhabited by the Scots. They are descendants of the bellicose Celts, whom even Emperor Hadrian could not

submit. So he ordered his soldiers to build a 120km/74.5 mile long stone wall, called Hadrian's Wall, which divided England from Scotland. The Scots are traditionalists. On occasions requiring formal regalia, the men wear a kilt, a skirt-like garment pleated at the sides and back but flat at the front which comes in numerous tartan patterns. There is a famous legend about a prehistoric monster said to live in Loch Ness. Does Nessie really exist or are the Scots simply brilliant storytellers? In any case, the Britons are renowned for their dry humour. Ireland is nicknamed "Emerald Island" – it consists of rolling pastures dipped in clouds and there is a lot of rainfall. The Irish economy is strong in cattle breeding and the export of butter and milk. The entire coastline of Ireland is characterised by cliffs. Only the northwestern part of the island belongs to the UK, the rest is an independent nation centred

around the capital, Dublin. It is lovingly called Eire. The Irish love music and are well known for their folk music. Equally famous and popular is the dark ale brewed here, called Guinness.

The Royal Couple attending the celebrations for the opening of parliament.

Tower Bridge in London was built close to the tower, the city's gaol. The old dockyards on the other side of the Thames have recently been restructured. Big Ben is also close by.

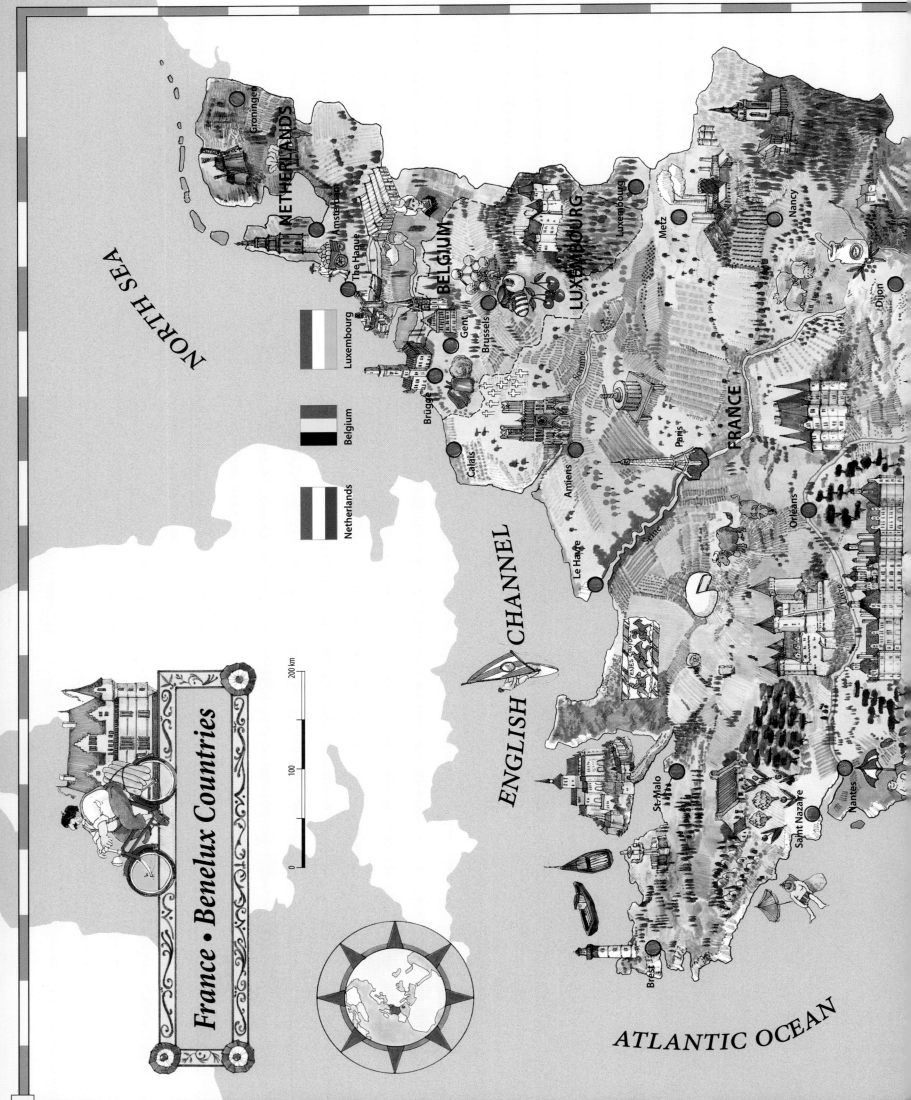

NORTH SEA

Groningen

NETHERLANDS

Amsterdam

The Hague

BELGIUM

Gent

Brussels

Brügge

Calais

Amiens

Le Havre

Seine

LUXEMBOURG

Luxembourg

Metz

Nancy

Dijon

FRANCE

Paris

Somme

Orleans

Loire

ENGLISH CHANNEL

St-Malo

Saint Nazaire

Nantes

Brest

ATLANTIC OCEAN

Luxembourg

Belgium

Netherlands

France • Benelux Countries

200 km

100

0

France
Monaco

Lake Geneva

ALPS

Rhône

Saône

Lyon

Grenoble

MONACO

Nice

Clermont-Ferrand

Nîmes

Toulon

Marseille

Rhône

MEDITERRANEAN

Garonne

Bordeaux

Lourdes

Pyrenees

Corsica (FRANCE)

Bastia

Mountainous Corsica with its beautiful beaches belongs to France. It is here that Napoleon was born.

France is central Europe's largest country. Its shape slightly reminds one of an old coffee pot, with the spout pointing towards the Atlantic, the handle just beginning in the Mediterranean, and its base on the border to Spain. The western part of France is relatively flat. Towards the east, the French flatlands join into a low mountain range. Next comes the broad Rhône valley on the other side of which the Alps rise up. Mont Blanc, with 4800 metres/15 744 feet the highest mountain of the Alps, is part of France. The Alps make up the natural border to Switzerland and Italy. The border to Spain is marked by the Pyrenee Mountains. At the foot of this mountain range lies Lourdes, a famous pilgrimage site. The Mediterranean coast called Côte d'Azur, is a popular holiday destination. Marseille has a huge port; Nice is renowned for its glamorous beach life; and Cannes every year hosts a large film festival. The Camargue is the area where the Rhône joins into the sea; it is famous for its wild horses and swarms of pink flamingos living by the lakes and ponds. France is a country rich in cultural heritage – there's the famous cathedral of Reims and the magnificent castles along the Loire such as Chambord, situated in a large wood which once was the king's hunting ground. France is famous for its

fashion design and perfumes, its exquisite cuisine and wines. Paris, the capital, is the country's cultural and economic centre. The Louvre museum and Eiffel tower are famous Paris landmarks.

The capital of the kingdom of the Netherlands is The Hague; Amsterdam is the cultural centre. Rotterdam has

the largest port in Europe. The Dutch are a seafaring people who grew to wealth by overseas trading.

Industry, agriculture, and natural-gas resources secure the nation's main income. Belgium, which lies between France and the Netherlands, was also industrialised fairly early and is an equally important exporting country. It is a kingdom with many beautiful old cities, including the magnificent capital Brussels. In Belgium, the official languages are French and Dutch. Luxembourg is a small state with steel and iron industry and an important financial centre. People here speak Luxembourgian, French, and German.

Typically Dutch windmills in Kinderdijk.

Brussels market square with its Gothic town hall and Baroque facades.

15

Situated right in the Pyrenees, which stretch between France and the Iberian Peninsula, the dwarf state Andorra nestles in the scraggy mountains. However, the main part of this mountain range belongs to Spain which shares the sunny peninsula with its neighbour Portugal. For 600 years, this area was ruled by the Romans. Then the Moors, an Arab people from North Africa, conquered the land. They stayed for 800 years, building ornate palaces such as the Alhambra in Granada. The Spanish and Portuguese people were very audacious seafarers. In 1492, Columbus discovered America – he was travelling on behalf of the Spanish king. In 1498, Portuguese discoverer Vasco da Gama finally found the much sought-after sea route to India. The Spanish capital Madrid lies on an elevated plain surrounded by mountains. This is the country where once Don Quixote warred against the windmills. Esparto grows here, a grass species from which mats, hats, and carpets are manufactured. Along the Mediterranean, fruit and vegetables are grown in huge fields. The grapes, spoilt by sun, make for some excellent wines. Sherry is a refined wine from southern Spain and is enjoyed throughout the world. Spain produces steel, ships, chemical products, and fabrics. On the north-eastern coast, in the region called Catalonia, lies Barcelona, an economic and cultural centre. Spain boasts of a coastline plus numerous beautiful islands that attract tourists from all over Europe. Typically Spanish are bullfights, presented by toreros, and flamenco, an expressive dance accompanied by guitar, vocals, and castanets. Portugal lies on the western coast of the Iberian Peninsula. It was a very wealthy country while it still had its colonies in overseas. Lisbon, the capital, still reverberates its former grandeur. Today, Portugal's economy mainly relies on agriculture and tourism. The south coast is characterised by beautiful long beaches. In the north, the famous port wine is produced, then stored in oak barrels for many years and finally exported all over the world.

Ávila is the highest city of Spain and towers on a hill above Rio Adaja river like a huge fortress. It was a strategically important site during the fights against the Moors.

Spain · Portugal

Bilbao

PYRENEES ANDORRA

Ebro

rgos

Barcelona

BALEARIC ISLANDS

Menorca

Majorca

Madrid

Toledo

Ibiza

MEDITERRANEAN

Formentera

Cartagena

Granada

Málaga

Madeira is the main island of an archipelago in the Atlantic Ocean which the Portuguese discovered in 1419. Alongside Madeira, Porto Santo, the Desertas, and the Selvagens belong to this group. Tourists adore Madeira, especially its magnificent gardens and terraces and the picturesque capital, Funchal.

The Azores were also discovered by Portuguese seafarers. This island group has volcanic origins. The climate is mild but every now and then stormy winds brush over the land.

500 km/310 miles off the Northwest-African coast lies an idyll of islands. Only seven of the Canary Islands, which total 13, are inhabited. These are: Fuerteventura; Gomera; Hierro; the blossoming island of Tenerife; the volcanic island Gran Canaria with its mile-long sand dunes and canyons; wild Lanzarote, which is covered in lava fields, tuff, and volcanic ashes, has fiery hills and a ground hot enough to fry eggs on; and La Palma, where the world's largest volcanic crater can be visited.

Andorra   Portugal   Spain

Madeira (PORTUGAL)

Azores (PORTUGAL)

Corvo

Graciosa

Flores

Faial

Terceira

Sao Jorge

Pico

Sao Miguel

Santa Maria

Azores

Madeira

Canary Islands

Canary Islands (SPAIN)

La Palma

Lanzarote

Tenerife

Gran Canaria

Gomera

Hierro

Fuerteventura

ALPS

Drau

Danube

Ljubljana

SLOVENIA

Triest

Zagreb

CROATIA

WOJW

Milan

Turin

Verona

Po

Venice

Ravenna

Genoa

SAN MARINO

Zadar

BOSNIA-
HERZEGOVINA

Pisa

Florence

Livorno

Ancona

San Marino

Sarajevo

Split

Mostar

ITALY

ADRIATIC

MON

Podgorica

Rome

VATICAN CITY

APENNINES

Dubrovník

Lake

Vatican
City

Montenegro

A

Bari

SARDINIA

Italy

Naples

Albania

Taranto

Tira

Cagliari

MEDITERRANEAN

Greece

SICILY

Palermo

Messina

Macedonia

Reggio di
Calabria

Siracusa

Italy has the unmistakable shape of a boot. The
Apennine mountain range spreads across a large
part of the country. To the north, the Alps mark
the border. Rome, the capital city, used to be the
centre of the Roman Empire. All over Italy remains
from the epoch can be found. Italy is also famous
as the country where opera music was invented.
Italy is densely populated. In the north there are
large metropolises with major industrial branches
such as steel, chemistry, and textiles, but there are
also several car manufacturers: Fiat, Alfa Romeo, and
Ferrari. Italy is the world's biggest wine exporting
country. In the poorer south, agriculture is the
main means of income. Several islands belong
to Italy: Elba and Ischia, Sardinia in the west and
Sicily at the tip of the boot. Malta, however, is an
independent state and part of the British Common-
wealth. San Marino in the northwest
and the Vatican State are also
independent city states.
East of Italy, on the Adriatic coast,
lies former Yugoslavia whose coastline dotted with cypress, pine and
palm trees is the perfect destination for
tourists yearning for some sun.

Malta

MALTA

St Peter's Cathedral is situated in the world's smallest
independent state, the Vatican. The church state in the centre
of Rome has its own government and own stamps, which are
favourite collectors' items. The head of state is the Pope.

Slovenia

Bosnia-Herzegovina

Croatia

Serbia

0   100   200 km

Italy • Greece • Southern Slavic States

Sad

Belgrade

Danube

BULGARIA

RBIA

GRO

Varna

Bulgaria

Sofia

Burgas

Skopje

Plovdiv

MACEDONIA

Maric

BALKAN

Lake Ohrid

Lake Presna

Thessaly

GREECE

AEGEAN

Athens

Crete

Irakleion

Rhodes

Greek god, Zeus, with his symbol, an eagle.

For many years, the different peoples that constituted Yugoslavia lived together peacefully. But then civil war erupted and a number of independent states were established. Serbia/Montenegro has some flat coast and lowlands in the north, but the major part of the country is mountainous and craggy. Slovenia, Croatia, and Bosnia-Herzegovina to the northwest are more fertile. Albania lies on the Adriatic, bordering on Greece towards the south. For many years, Albania and its capital Tirana were as politically secluded as they are geographically, with jagged mountain ranges to the north, east, and south. The coastline, a strip of alluvial land, is used for agriculture. Bulgaria is neighboured by Serbia to the west, Rumania to the north, and Greece and Turkey to the south. Its capital is Sofia. The Balkan mountains extend through central Bulgaria. To the east lies the Black Sea with beautiful beaches luring many holiday makers. Corn, fruit, wine, tobacco, sunflowers, and strawberries are grown in Bulgaria. Roses are used to produce the famous fragrances. Natural resources include coal, petroleum, lead, and zinc.

The Greek Peninsula consists of the Peloponnese that looks like a hand and the large island of Crete, which is far out in the Mediterranean. To the north, Greece borders on Albania, Macedonia, and Bulgaria. Greece is the cradle of western civilisation. Its philosophy, science, literature, architecture, and art have vitally influenced all of Europe. In the capital Athens as well as all over the country there are numerous ancient ruins. Alongside its multifaceted culture, Greece is also popular for its beautiful coasts and charming islands.

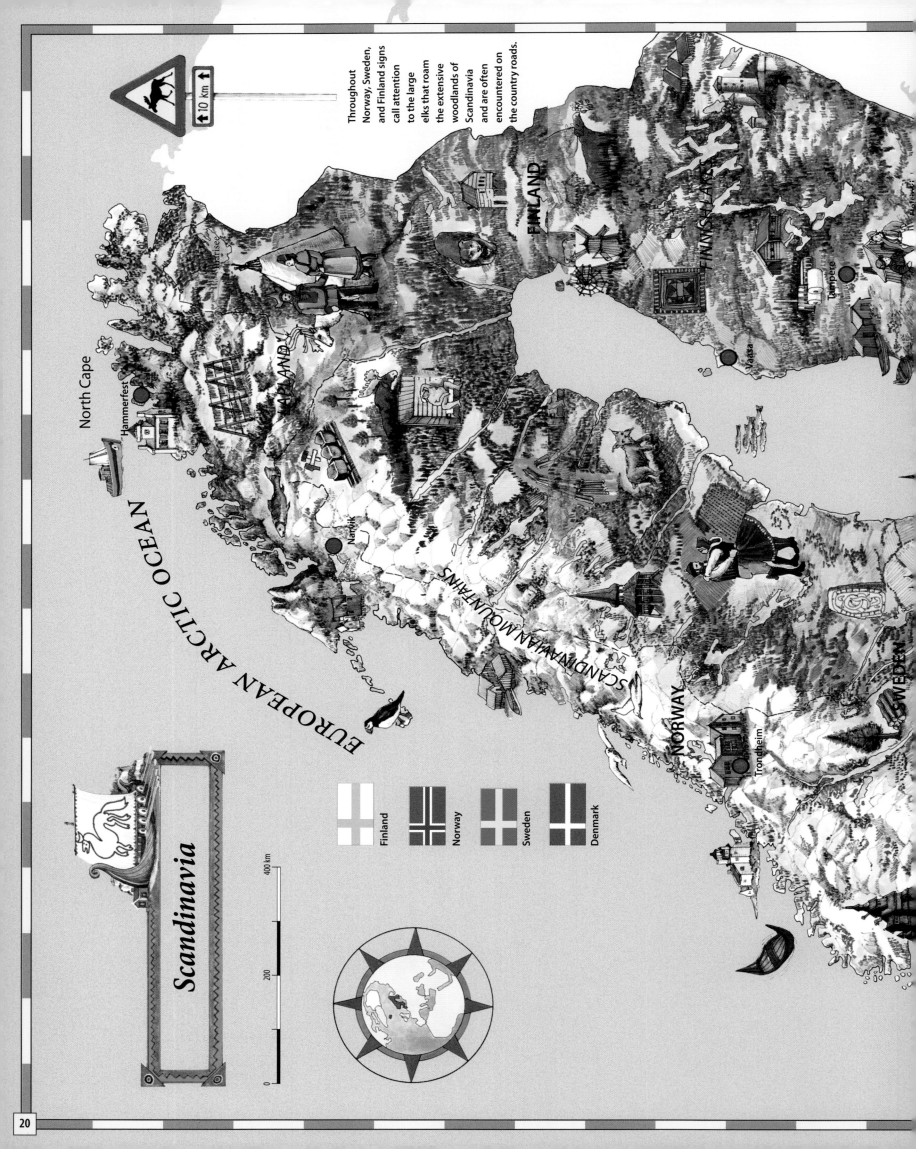

Scandinavia

Throughout Norway, Sweden, and Finland signs call attention to the large elks that roam the extensive woodlands of Scandinavia and are often encountered on the country roads.

10 km

EUROPEAN ARCTIC OCEAN

North Cape

Hammerfest

LAPLAND

Narvik

SCANDINAVIAN MOUNTAINS

NORWAY

Trondheim

SWEDEN

FINLAND

FINNISH LAKE

Vaasa

Tampere

Finland

Norway

Sweden

Denmark

400 km

200

0

their living mainly with fishing, agriculture, and timber. The various countries are very different. Denmark, which consists of Jutland and 500 islands of varying sizes, is very flat. Agriculture and stock raising, the production of butter and other dairy products are an important business branch. Children from all over the world delight in playing with Lego bricks, a Danish product. Norway, on the other hand, is very mountainous and thus unsuitable for agriculture. In fact, Norway has to import many foodstuffs. But the worthy descendants of the Vikings have a powerful fleet of trade vessels. Off the wildly romantic Norwegian coast with its long fjords, right in the North Sea, petroleum and natural gas are exploited.

Neighbouring Sweden is characterised by forests, mountains, lakes, and flat sandy beaches. It is a wealthy country rich in ore, producing timber, automobiles, machines, chemical products, and paper.

No other country has as many lakes as Finland – more than 55 000 water bodies surrounded by extensive woodlands. The lakes remained after the Ice Age glaciers had melted. The sauna was invented in Finland, where timber is produced alongside ships, machinery, and industrial plants. Telecommunication and consumer electronics such as mobile phones are also important for the economy.

The north of Europe is made up of the Scandinavian countries Denmark, Norway, Sweden, Finland, and the island Iceland. In Finland, both Finnish and Swedish are spoken. The bitterly cold north with its snowy landscape is populated by Laplanders, also called Sami. They raise reindeer, and a small part of them still lives a nomadic life, always on the move with large reindeer herds, just like hundreds of years ago. Up in the very north the sun does not go down completely at night during the summer, so it remains light enough to read outdoors, but during the winter it is dark for days on end. The Scandinavians make

Kronborg Castle in Denmark is where William Shakespeare's drama "Hamlet" unfolds.

ICELAND

Iceland lies approximately 1100 km/683 miles off the Norwegian coast. Its arid elevated plain in the island centre is characterised by more than 100 volcanoes, lava fields, and large glaciers. The steaming hot water form the springs and geysers is used to heat towns and greenhouses.

Reykjavik

0   200   400   600 km

Aland Isles

BALTIC SEA

Gotland

Stockholm

Kalmar

Bornholm

Karlstadt

Lake Vätter

Malmö

Göteborg

Copenhagen

Lake Vänder

Oslo

Arhus

DENMARK

NORTH SEA

WHITE SEA

Rapuesk Reservoir

Lake Onega

RUSSIA

Moscow

Lake Ladoga

Saint Petersburg

Smolensk

Twer

Vitebsk

ESTONIA

Tallinn

LATVIA

Daugava

Minsk

Riga

Daugava

BELARUS

Vilnius

LITHUANIA

RUSSIA

Klaipeda

Brest

BALTIC SEA

Warsaw

Vistula

POLAND

Lodz

Poland · Czech Republic · Slovakia · Hungary ·
Romania · Baltic States · Russia ·
Belarus · Moldavia · Ukraine

Flags:

Poland

Czech Republic

Romania

Hungary

Slovakia

Estonia

Latvia

Lithuania

1000 km

500

0

Poland lies between the Baltic Sea and the
Carpathian Mountains. Agriculture and
industry are equally important: natural resources
in Silesia include bituminous coal, brown coal,
and ores which are used for the production of
machines, automobiles, and in the metalworking
industry. Locomotives and ships are built in
Poland. Poland's culture contributed to the Western
civilisation; its capital is Warsaw; Krakow has
one of the oldest universities in Europe. When
the Archbishop of Krakow was elected Pope John
Paul, this was a boost for the national spirit.
The Czech Republic, which borders on Germany
and Poland, is halfway encircled by the Bavarian
and Upper Palatinate Forests, the Ore and the
Sudeten Mountains. The highlands are rich in
brown and bituminous coal, used for industrial
branches such as steel, machine, and automobile
production, and the chemical industry.

Bohemia has a long-standing tradition in manufacturing glassware and jewellery. Slovakia, which is also defined by its mountains, was only industrialised after the Second World War. Both Czechia and Slovakia still have a lot of agriculture and stock breeding. The countries used to be united as Czechoslovakia, a nation rich in cultural traditions. Beautiful Prague is the capital of Czechia and is one of Europe's oldest university towns. Travelling down the Danube from the Slovakian capital Bratislava, one reaches the Hungarian capital, Budapest. The Chain Bridge connects the two parts of

the city, Buda and Pest. Beyond Budapest, the extensive steppe called Puszta begins. The landscape of Hungary is determined by highlands in the popular Lake Balaton area and the great Hungarian lowlands which extend along the rivers Danube and Tisza. There is a lot of agriculture in Hungary as well as the production of finished goods. The white Tokajer and various red wines are highly renowned. The Hungarians speak a language that was introduced by the Magyar people and is related to Finnish. East of Hungary lies Romania whose people speak a language very like Italian because Romania was part of the Roman Empire for a good 200 years. The Carpathians

In Czechia and Slovakia, there are numerous old castles such as Karlstein Castle.

are a semi-circular mountain range in which legendary Count Dracula roamed. They separate the Transylvanian Highlands in the west of Romania from the flatlands in the east which extend to the Black Sea. The kingdom of Romania with its capital Bucharest used to be a thriving agricultural nation but today, after many years of mismanagement, it is very impoverished. On the northern coast of the Black Sea lies the

Crimean Peninsula which belongs to the Ukraine. It used to be part of the Soviet Union, which stretched from the Polish border right through to China and the Pacific Ocean and from the Black Sea north to the cold Polar regions. The Ural Mountains separate the European part of Russia with its capital Moscow and the former csar's residence town, St. Petersburg, from Asia. A wide variety of peoples made up the Soviet Union, the transport routes were extremely long, and many areas, especially in the Asian part, were sparsely inhabited and hard to reach. The harsh climate with the long cold winters made things even more difficult – this huge empire could no longer be ruled from Moscow. When industrialisation failed to bring the coveted wealth and the run-down agricultural system could no longer feed all the people, the Soviet Union broke apart into various small states.

Three great Russians that made history: Czar Peter the Great, Vladimir Iljitsch Lenin, and Michail Gorbatchev.

Russia

Belarus

Moldova

Ukraine

CAUCASIAN MOUNTAINS
ASOV SEA
CRIMEA
BLACK SEA
UKRAINE
MOLDOVA
ROMANIA
HUNGARY
PUSZTA
SLOVAKIA

Charkow
Dnjepropetrowsk
Kiev
Dnjepr
Odessa
Sevastopol
L'viv
Chistnau
Brasov
Bukarest
Krakov
Bratislava
Bucharest
Danube

Some of the remotest and most inhospitable countries of the earth are found in North Asia: Siberia, Mongolia, and Tibet. In Siberia, during the winter it can get as cold as –60°C/–76°F. Three quarters of the soil there remain frozen throughout the year. This is where the Russians would send their prisoners until only recently; they had to help exploit the wealth of natural resources such as iron ore, coal, petroleum, and timber. The indigenous peoples of Siberia, the Chukotka, Evenk, and Yakut, are related to the Native Americans, whose forebears migrated via the Bering Strait from North Asia to Alaska. Siberia is only very scarcely populated because the harsh climate makes living conditions very difficult. The same can be said of Mongolia, the land of famous warrior, Genghis Khan. It consists mainly of steppe and the Gobi Desert. To the west towers a range of mountains as high as 4000m/13.120 feet. The steppe is ideal grazing land for horses, cattle, sheep, goats, and camels. Even today, nomads live in easy to build round tents, called yurt. They follow their herds on their search for food. The land is not suited for agriculture and there has not been much industrialisation

This mural from a temple in Ladakh is nearly 1000 years old. It shows a soldier taking a captive.

yet. The government in the capital of Ulan Bator has not managed to make its population of 2.5 million settle down. The main Mongolian creed is Tibetan Buddhism, adopted from their neighbours to the southwest. The communists tried to ban this creed. Before it was controlled by China, Tibet was a religious state run by its head, the Dalai Lama. It was very influential from China to Nepal and Bhutan in the Himalayas. The highest region on earth, Tibet is also called "The Roof of the World". The kingdom of Bhutan is very isolated. The king has announced elections, wishing to introduce democracy. Lama monks preserve the national traditions. Nepal is a monarchy with 24 million inhabitants; its capital

Kathmandu lies high up in the Himalayas. The standard of living is fairly low and the medical supply wanting. The Nepalese live from agriculture, but the soil is barren and the harvest is meagre. China is a very mountainous country. Counting a population of over 1 billion people, it is the world's most densely populated nation. Most people live in the flatlands to the east, extending along the two rivers Huang-ho and Yangtze Kiang. Chinese culture reached a peak many

centuries ago. During the times of the Chinese Empire, magnificent buildings were constructed in Beijing and the Chinese produced highly influential works in the fields of philosophy, literature, and painting. Their fine bone china and silk fabrics are renowned all over the world. The Chinese invented

Potala is the Dalai Lama's former winter residence in the Tibetan capital of Lhasa.

Russia

Georgia

Armenia

Azerbaijan

Uzbekistan

Kazakhstan

Turkmenistan

Tajikistan

Kyrgyzstan

Nepal

Bhutan

Japan

North Korea

South Korea

0   1000   2000 km

Jakutsk

Irkutsk

Ulan Bator

MONGOLIA

GOBI DESERT

Harbin

Komsomolsk

Amur

Lena

Vladivostok

NORTH KOREA

Pyongyang

Seoul

SOUTH KOREA

JAPAN

Tokyo

PACIFIC OCEAN

Xian

Yangtze Kiang

PEOPLE'S REPUBLIC OF CHINA

Shanghai

Mongolia

People's Republic of China

Taipeh

TAIWAN

Hong Kong

Taiwan

both paper and gunpowder. To protect themselves against the Mongolians, they constructed a 5000 km/ 3100 mile long wall. The Chinese have a very complex script consisting of more than 30 000 signs. Of these, 4000 are used for daily communication. When the Communists came to power in 1949, they turned China into a state of workers and farmers, wantonly destroying many ancient works of art. Economy is based on agriculture and consumer goods. The country has rich deposits of coal, iron, and petroleum. The peninsula Korea to the east of China is very much influenced by Chinese culture. It is divided into the communist northern and the capitalist southern part. The capitals are Pyongyang in the north and Seoul in the south. Korea and Japan are part of the Pacific Ring of Fire, called thus due to its many volcanoes. Japan is an island with more volcanoes than any other country on earth – every year, about 5000 earthquakes are registered. With 130 million inhabitants, the island is very densely populated. There is some agriculture though the many industrial branches have turned Japan into one of the richest countries of the world. The Japanese combine industrial progress with a deep sense of tradition. Many companies are organised like extended families. Employees virtually stay with their company for their entire working career and spend much of their leisure time with colleagues.

Only few people were allowed inside the "Forbidden City", the palace of the Chinese Emperor.

Luzon

Myanmar (Burma)

Laos

Philippines

East Timor

Hanoi

MYANMAR
(BURMA)

LAOS

Vientiane

Thailand

Cambodia

Manila

PHILIPPINES

THAILAND

VIETNAM

Vietnam

Yangon

Palawan

Mindanao

Bangkok

Phnom Penh

CAMBODIA

SOUTH CHINA SEA

BRUNEI

Manado

Malaysia

MALAYSIA

SARAWAK

Molukkes

Singapore

KALIMANTAN
(BORNEO)

Sulawesi
(Celebes)

Kuala Lumpur

INDONESIA

Indonesia

Singapore

SINGAPORE

Banjarmasin

Brunei

Sumbawa

Flores

EAST TIMOR

SUMATRA

Jakarta

Java

Bali

Lombok

Sumba

Timor

INDIAN OCEAN

The world's largest earth-quake zone starts in Myanmar, in western Southeast Asia, and extends over all of East and Southeast Asia, New Guinea, New Zealand, and Polynesia, right through to the west coast of the USA. The frequent quakes are mainly caused by plate tectonics, movements along the fault lines of the earth's plates, as well as by the numerous volcanoes. Indonesia alone has 300 volcanoes, of which 100 are still active. The entire Pacific Basin is also referred to as "Earth's Ring of Fire". Southeast Asia, Papua-New Guinea, and northern Australia are covered with tropical rain forest. Many kinds of timber grow

here, such as bamboo, rattan, teak, and mahogany. Unfortunately, deforestation is increasing so fast that the forests cannot re-grow again properly. The coastlines are characterised by mangroves with their prop roots sticking out of the soil. They were the perfect hiding grounds for pirates who there could not be discovered from the open sea. All over Southeast Asia, the colonial rulers laid out plantations with useful plants such as gummi elasticum, used for rubber production, coffee, tea, sugar cane, cloves, vanilla, and cinnamon. Today, the locals run

In the mythology of Bali, the Barong, a remote relative of the Chinese New Year's Lion, personifies earth's positive powers.
Between 1113 and 1150, the powerful Khmer dynasty built the Hindu temple of Angor Wat, Cambodia. This was the place to come and worship the gods and also the burial site of the great King Suryavarman II. The highest tower of the holy complex is 65m/213 feet high. A 200m/656 feet wide moat encircles the temple.

Perth

PACIFIC OCEAN

0   500   1000   1500 km

RIAN JAYA

PAPUA NEW GUINEA

Papua New Guinea

Australia

New Zealand

GREAT DIVIDING RANGE

AUSTRALIA

GREAT VICTORIA DESERT

Brisbane

Sydney

Canberra

Adelaide

Melbourne

TASMANIA

NEW ZEALAND

Hobart

Wellington

the plantations themselves. There are also many natural resources such as petroleum, natural gas, and tin. The jungle makes exploiting the natural resources rather difficult, though. In most countries the standard of living is not as high as might be expected judging the wealth in natural riches. There are two exceptions: Singapore, a city state that is an important banking centre and has one of the world's largest ports, and the Sultanate Brunei on the island of Borneo, where the world's richest man lives. Some states, such as Myanmar, Cambodia, Laos, and Vietnam, are still affected by the consequences of colonialism and civil wars. The increasing population is another problem. Towards the end of the 20th century, 340 million people lived in Southeast Asia and only about 40 million in New Guinea, Australia, and New Zealand. After the Second World War, the European colonialists retreated from Southeast Asia; in New Zealand, the indigenous people, the Maori, were integrated into the white society. In Australia, on the other hand, the native Aborigines were nearly entirely extinct – only approximately 150 000 natives have remained. In the Australian Alps in the south there is enough snow to go skiing. But what the Australians enjoy even more is surfing the waves along their many beautiful beaches.

Elaborately carved pantry house of the Maori people in New Zealand.

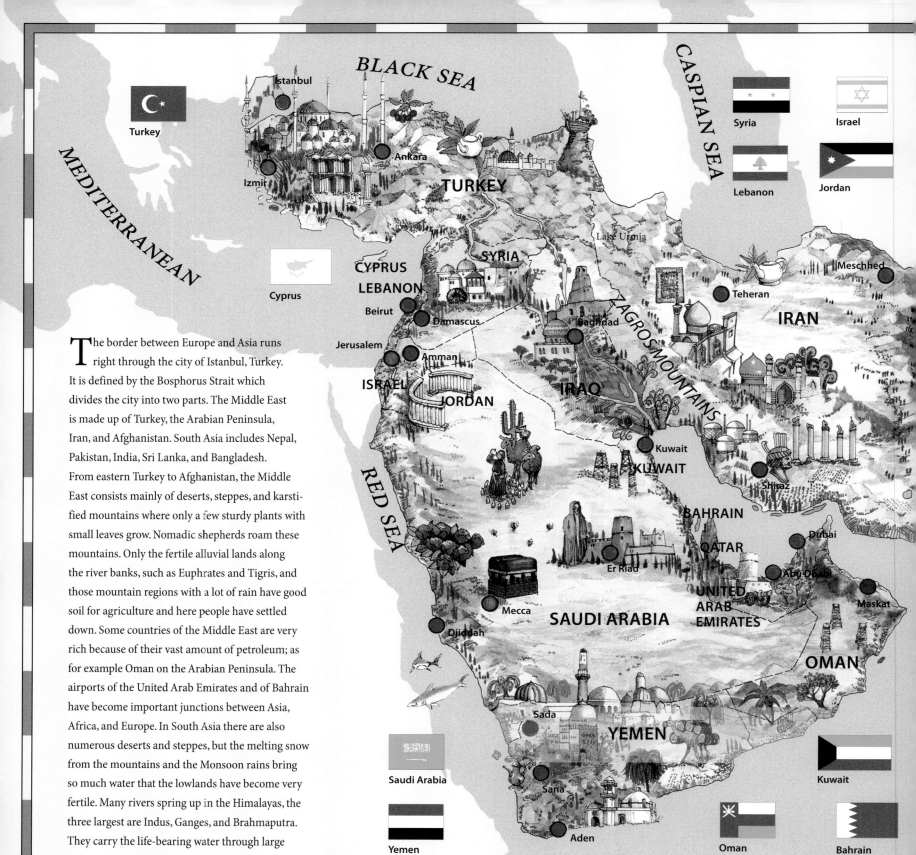

BLACK SEA

CASPIAN SEA

MEDITERRANEAN

RED SEA

Turkey

Istanbul
Izmit
Ankara

TURKEY

CYPRUS
Cyprus

SYRIA
LEBANON
Beirut
Damascus

Jerusalem
ISRAEL
Amman

JORDAN

IRAQ
Baghdad

Lake Urmia

ZAGROS MOUNTAINS

Teheran

IRAN

Meschhed

Kuwait
KUWAIT

Shiraz

BAHRAIN
QATAR

Dubai

Abu Dhabi

Er Riad

UNITED
ARAB
EMIRATES

Maskat

Mecca

SAUDI ARABIA

OMAN

Djiddah

Sada

YEMEN

Sana

Aden

Syria
Israel
Lebanon
Jordan

Saudi Arabia
Yemen

Kuwait
Oman
Bahrain
United Arab Emirates
Qatar

The border between Europe and Asia runs right through the city of Istanbul, Turkey. It is defined by the Bosphorus Strait which divides the city into two parts. The Middle East is made up of Turkey, the Arabian Peninsula, Iran, and Afghanistan. South Asia includes Nepal, Pakistan, India, Sri Lanka, and Bangladesh. From eastern Turkey to Afghanistan, the Middle East consists mainly of deserts, steppes, and karstified mountains where only a few sturdy plants with small leaves grow. Nomadic shepherds roam these mountains. Only the fertile alluvial lands along the river banks, such as Euphrates and Tigris, and those mountain regions with a lot of rain have good soil for agriculture and here people have settled down. Some countries of the Middle East are very rich because of their vast amount of petroleum; as for example Oman on the Arabian Peninsula. The airports of the United Arab Emirates and of Bahrain have become important junctions between Asia, Africa, and Europe. In South Asia there are also numerous deserts and steppes, but the melting snow from the mountains and the Monsoon rains bring so much water that the lowlands have become very fertile. Many rivers spring up in the Himalayas, the three largest are Indus, Ganges, and Brahmaputra. They carry the life-bearing water through large areas of the continent. Monsoon is the wind in India which changes according to the season. In summer, the wind brings in warm and damp air mass from the Indian ocean. If it comes too late, the fields dry up and there's a danger of famines. But the Monsoon isn't always a blessing. Often the rainfalls are so heavy that the rivers flood the land, dragging with them houses, people, and livestock. The best-known country of South

In 70 AD the Romans destroyed Jerusalem. What remains is the so-called Wailing Wall which used to be part of the enclosure of the Hebrew temple complex. Jews have come here since the Middle Ages to seek comfort in prayer. In 638, the Arabs constructed a holy site for the Islam on the other side of the wall, the Dome of the Rock.

Asia is India. Its cultural tradition goes back many thousands of years during which fabulous works of art have been created: magnificent temples with refined stone sculptures, imposing palaces, and the literary language Sanskrit. Religion is an important factor in Indian everyday life. 85% of the population are Hindi, then there are Muslims and Buddhists.

Iran

Iraq

Afghanistan

Pakistan

India

Sri Lanka

Nepal

Bhutan

Bangladesh

Middle East • South Asia

0   500   1000 km

AFGHANISTAN

HINDU KUSH

Kabul

Islamabad

HIMALAYAS

PAKISTAN

Indus

Delhi

NEPAL

Kathmandu

BHUTAN

Thimbu

Brahmaputra

Gauhati

Karachi

Ganges

Dhaka

BANGLADESH

INDIA

Narmada

Calcutta

Mumbai
(Bombay)

Madras

INDIAN OCEAN

Sri Lanka

Colombo

Mahatma Gandhi (1869–1948) was the leader of the Indian independence movement.

Hinduism categorises people according to their social and professional backgrounds. One is born into the so-called caste and belongs to it throughout one's life. In other words, at birth it is decided whether one is a member of the upper or the lower classes; whether one will remain rich or poor. India is a tropical country with a fairly hot climate. Large parts of the country are covered with rain forests and jungles, savannah and steppe; lions, tigers, leopards, and elephants still roam free here. The main part of the population lives in the fertile cuontryside and in the increasingly growing metropolises where iron and steel industry as well as textile fabrication promise employment. But poverty can also be exceedingly harsh. All in all, the standard of living in South Asia is compara-tively low. Population growth is an issue in this region. For example, the population of relatively small Pakistan grows by 2 million every year.

Taj Mahal in the north Indian town of Agra is built entirely out of white marble and famous throughout the world. Mogul king Shash Jahan had it constructed in 1633 as a tomb for his deceased favourite wife. The burial place itself is 65m/213 feet high, but it is only a part of the extensive complex with forecourt and gardens, situated on the Yamuna river.

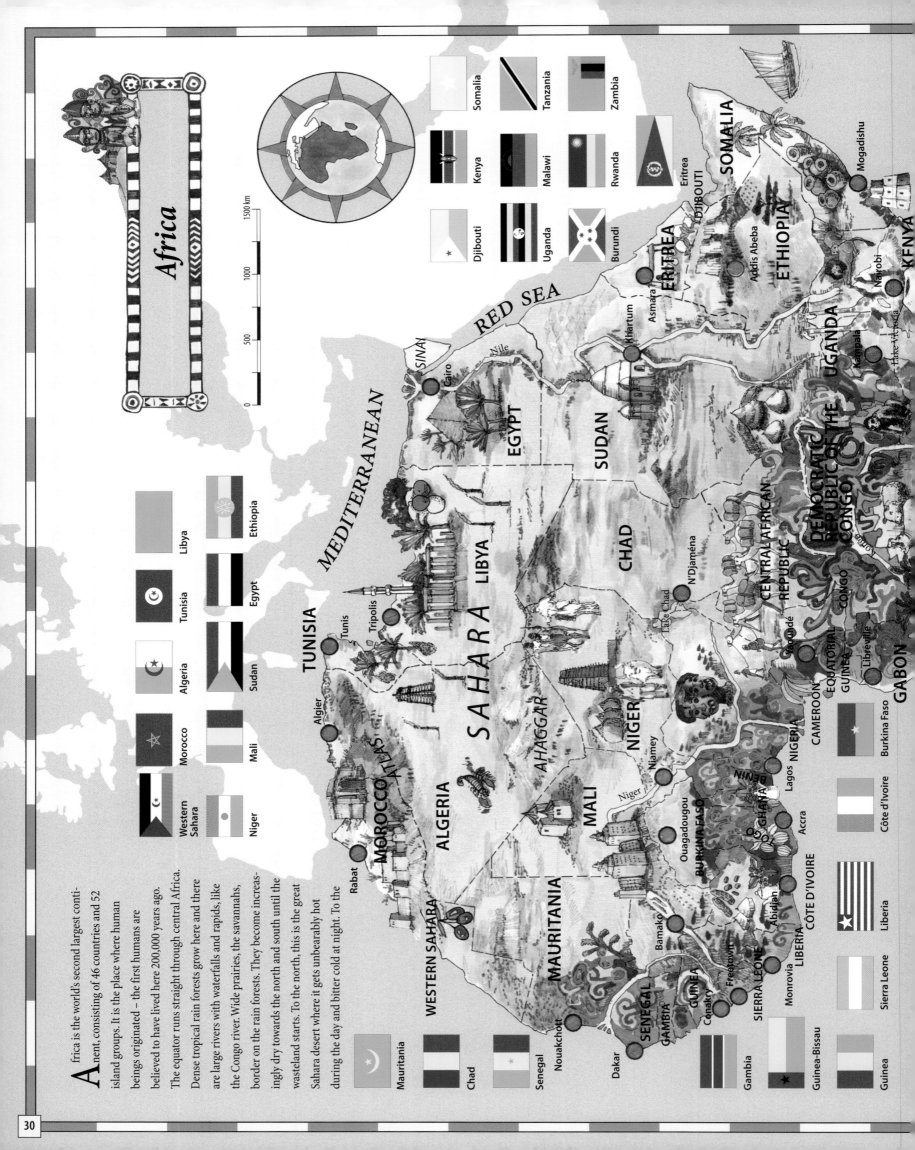

Africa

Africa is the world's second largest continent, consisting of 46 countries and 52 island groups. It is the place where human beings originated – the first humans are believed to have lived here 200,000 years ago. The equator runs straight through central Africa. Dense tropical rain forests grow here and there are large rivers with waterfalls and rapids, like the Congo river. Wide prairies, the savannahs, border on the rain forests. They become increasingly dry towards the north and south until the wasteland starts. To the north, this is the great Sahara desert where it gets unbearably hot during the day and bitter cold at night. To the

1500 km

1000

500

0

Somalia

Tanzania

Zambia

Kenya

Malawi

Rwanda

Eritrea

Djibouti

Uganda

Burundi

Libya

Ethiopia

Tunisia

Egypt

Algeria

Sudan

Morocco

Mali

Western Sahara

Niger

Mauritania

Chad

Senegal

Burkina Faso

Côte d'Ivoire

Liberia

Sierra Leone

Gambia

Guinea-Bissau

Guinea

MEDITERRANEAN

RED SEA

SINAI

Nile

Cairo

EGYPT

SUDAN

Khartum

Asmara

ERITREA

DJIBOUTI

Addis Abeba

ETHIOPIA

SOMALIA

Mogadishu

Nairobi

KENYA

Lake Victoria

Kampala

UGANDA

TUNISIA

Tunis

Tripolis

LIBYA

Algier

ATLAS

MOROCCO

Rabat

ALGERIA

SAHARA

AHAGGAR

CHAD

Lake Chad

N'Djaména

CENTRAL AFRICAN REPUBLIC

DEMOCRATIC REPUBLIC OF THE CONGO

Yaoundé

CAMEROON

EQUATORIAL GUINEA

CONGO

Libreville

GABON

NIGER

Niamey

Niger

NIGERIA

Lagos

BENIN

Ouagadougou

BURKINA FASO

GHANA

Accra

CÔTE D'IVOIRE

Abidjan

MALI

MAURITANIA

Nouakchott

WESTERN SAHARA

Bamako

SENEGAL

Dakar

GAMBIA

GUINEA

Conakry

SIERRA LEONE

Freetown

LIBERIA

Monrovia

30

MADAGASCAR

TANZANIA

Dodoma

Antananarivo

ANGOLA

Luanda

Malawisee

e Tanganjika

ZAMBIA

MALAWI

MOZAMBIQUE

ZIMBABWE

Lusaka

Victoria Falls

Bulawayo

Maputo

Sambesi

BOTSWANA

Gaborone

Johannesburg

SWAZILAND

LESOTHO

SOUTH AFRICA

NAMIBIA

Windhoek

KALAHARI

Cape Town

INDIAN OCEAN

ATLANTIC OCEAN

Congo

Zimbabwe

Comoros

Botswana

Madagascar

Swaziland

Lesotho

Mozambique

Namibia

South Africa

Angola

Togo

Nigeria

Central African Republic

Ghana

Benin

Cameroon

Gabon

Equatorial Guinea

Democratic Republic of the Congo

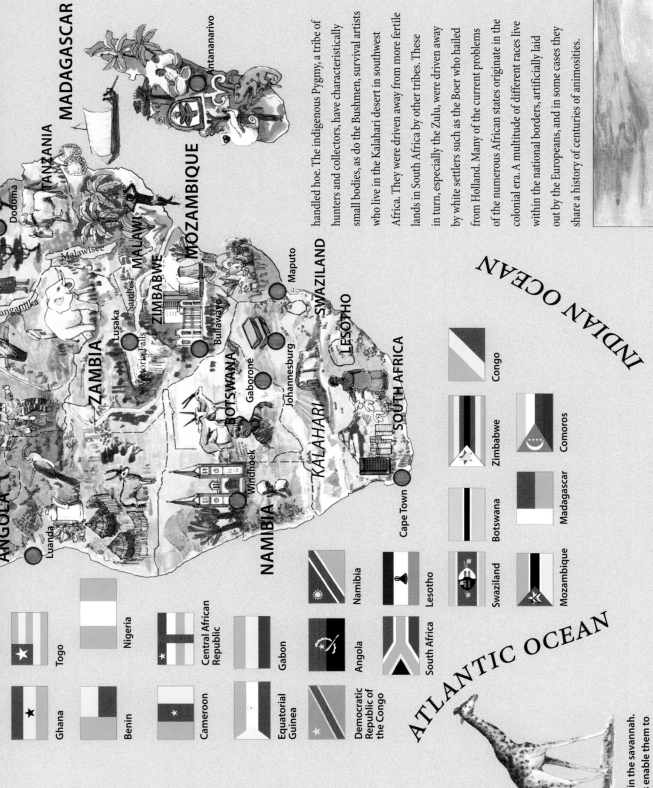

handled hoe. The indigenous Pygmy, a tribe of hunters and collectors, have characteristically small bodies, as do the Bushmen, survival artists who live in the Kalahari desert in southwest Africa. They were driven away from more fertile lands in South Africa by other tribes. These in turn, especially the Zulu, were driven away by white settlers such as the Boer who hailed from Holland. Many of the current problems of the numerous African states originate in the colonial era. A multitude of different races live within the national borders, artificially laid out by the Europeans, and in some cases they share a history of centuries of animosities.

Dromedaries have been used since time immemorial as a means of transport for merchants and travellers wishing to cross the Saharan desert. They are undemanding and fast, have great stamina and can make do without water for a very long time.

The pyramids of Giza where constructed c. 2500 BC. They are the tombs of the pharaohs Cheops and Cheophren, and together with the sphinx were one of the seven Wonders of the Ancient World. The sphinx is a guardian spirit, a lion's body with the head of a woman and a pharaoh's headdress.

The giraffes live in the savannah. Their long necks enable them to reach the high canopies of the trees. Here they can eat calmly with no rivals to worry about.

south, the sun glows over the Kalahari desert. Even further south, towards the Cape of Good Hope, the ocean determines the climate. In the winter it rains as much here as on the North-African coastline along the Mediterranean. Berbers and Arabs live in North Africa. In earlier centuries, the Twareg and the Berbers used to control the entire trade between the Ivory or Gold Coast of West Africa and Europe. They founded the trade centre Timbuktu in what today is Mali. The Twareg men wear an indigo coloured veil. This is to protect them from the dust swirled up when riding. When they ride through the desert on their camels, their blue tunics can be seen from afar. For centuries, the mighty Pharaohs ruled Egypt. This country is fed by the large river Nile, whose alluvial land is very fertile. Along the Niger river and in the lake districts of East Africa there were also very powerful realms such as that of the Ife, a Yoruba ethnic group, or the medieval Mutapa Empire. Huge volcanoes rise up in this lake district with famous Lake Victoria and Lake Tanganjika: snow-topped Kilimanjaro is 5895 m/19 335 feet high; Mount Kenya 5195 m/17 039 feet. In the arid savannah of Sudan or the neighbouring states Chad and Niger live the Fulbhe and Hausa, a pastoralist people who make do with whatever their livestock produce: meat, milk, leather, blood as a fortifier, cow dung as fuel and for covering the roofs of their houses. Big game like zebras, antelopes, and gnus graze in the damp savannah that extends towards the south. Various hunting tribes live here, such as the proud and beautiful Masai warriors who roam the lands following herds of wild game. Farmers have settled in the tropical rain forests of central Africa, tending the fields with their traditional short-

North America

Puerto Rico
Costa Rica
Barbados
Grenada
El Salvador
Cuba
Bahamas
Haiti
Dominican Republic
Jamaica

NEWFOUNDLAND
Halifax
Québec
Montreal
Ottawa
New York
Washington D.C.
Lake Ontario
Lake Huron
Niagara Falls
Lake Erie
Detroit
Lake Superior
Lake Michigan
Chicago
UNITED STATES

CANADA
Lake Winnipeg
Lake Athabasca
Great Bear Lake
Great Slave Lake
Mackenzie
ROCKY MOUNTAINS
Calgary
Vancouver
Portland
Great Salt Lake
Salt Lake City
Grand Canyon
Yukon
ALASKA

PACIFIC OCEAN

OCEAN

Belize
Panama

Canada
USA
Mexico
Guatemala
Honduras
Nicaragua

1500 km
1000
500
0

In 1914, the Panama Canal was completed. It had been dug through the narrowest stretch of land between South and North America and now marks the border between the two continents. When Christopher Columbus discovered America in 1492, he witnessed the high civilisation of the Maya people who had erected a huge realm in today's areas of Yucatan and Guatemala. The Mexican highlands were ruled by the Aztec.

cent works of art, and were excellent mathematicians and astronomers. The advent of the Spaniards craving for gold brought with it one of the most dreadful homicides in human history. The native Indians were killed, many of them perished from imported diseases. America was colonised by the Spanish, French, and British.

Today, a colourful variety of people lives in North America. Immigrants came here from all over the world. During the process of settling, the native Indians were dislodged and crowded into reservations.

The USA consist of 50 federal states and count among the richest nations of the world. The American president resides in the White House in the capital, Washington D.C. Along the west coast of North America, the Rocky Mountains stretch from north to south. The state of California with movie capital Hollywood and Silicon Valley, the cradle of the computer industry, is often shaken by earthquakes. Towards the east, the Great Plains extend where wheat and corn are harvested. Texas is characterised by petroleum exploitation and cattle breeding. To the south, tobacco and cotton are grown – formerly this work used to be done by African slaves. In the plateau of Arizona, the Colorado river has dug the 1800m/5904 feet deep Grand Canyon. Yellowstone National Park is noted for its 10 000 geysers, fountains up to 50m/164 feet high. Florida is defined by swamps populated by alligators, snakes, giant turtles, and manatees.

From Cape Canaveral in Florida, rockets with research satellites and spacecraft are launched into the orbit.

North of the United States lies Canada. Giant trees than can be up to 8 m/26 feet thick, such as Dougals and Hemlock fir or cedars, are cut down and transported by floating them down the rivers. Canada is the largest timber exporting country in the world. Modern machinery also help in agriculture and stock breeding, mining natural resources such as gold, platinum, and uranium, and exploiting petroleum. When a blizzard makes it impossible for a doctor to see his patient, he makes a diagnosis via satellite. In Canada, French and English are spoken. In the countries south of the USA, in Mexico and the seven smaller central American states, Spanish is the official language. The climate here is subtropical to tropical and plants can grow very high. Water lilies can be found with leaves 2 m/6.5 feet in diameter; sequoia trees can grow as high as 120 m/394 feet and as old as 1500 years. Cactus plants growing in the deserts can reach the height of a house. The society consists of a small, wealthy upper class and a large majority of poor people made up of Whites, Negroes, and Indigenous Native Americans. Gaining some moderate national wealth is disturbed by various factors from changing dictators or political unrest to erupting volcanoes with streams of lava and landslides. Peaceful and paradisiac Costa Rica stands out – the military has been abolished and the country thrives on the export of bananas and coffee.

Coffee, cocoa, indigo, cotton, and sugar cane are grown on the Caribbean Islands. Cuba is famed for its cigars, the Habanos, while Jamaica is known for rum and Reggae music. The Bahamas are an island paradise situated between Cuba and the Florida coast. All of the Caribbean islands are popular holiday destinations.

The Statue of Liberty in New York was presented to the US by France. 354 steps inside the statue lead to the platform located in the crown which offers a magnificent view of New York Harbor and the skyline of Manhattan.

Excerpt of a Miztec manuscript, an Indigenous Native American people from central America.

Maya cemetery on Yucatan Peninsula, Mexico.

The skyscrapers of Dallas, Texas, bear witness to the wealth gained through oil exploitation.

ATLANTIC

PUERTO RICO
San Juan
DOMINICAN REPUBLIC
Santo Domingo
HAITI
Port-au-Prince
BAHAMAS
Miami
Kingston
JAMAICA
CUBA
Havanna
Panama Canal
Panama
PANAMA
COSTA RICA
San José
Tegucigalpa
HONDURAS
Managua
NICARAGUA
San Salvador
EL SALVADOR
BELIZE
Belmopan
GUATEMALA
Guatemala
Vera Cruz
Acapulco
Mexiko City
Tampico
MEXICO
GULF OF MEXICO
New Orleans
Houston
Columbia
San Diego
Chihuahua
Rio Grande
Colorado

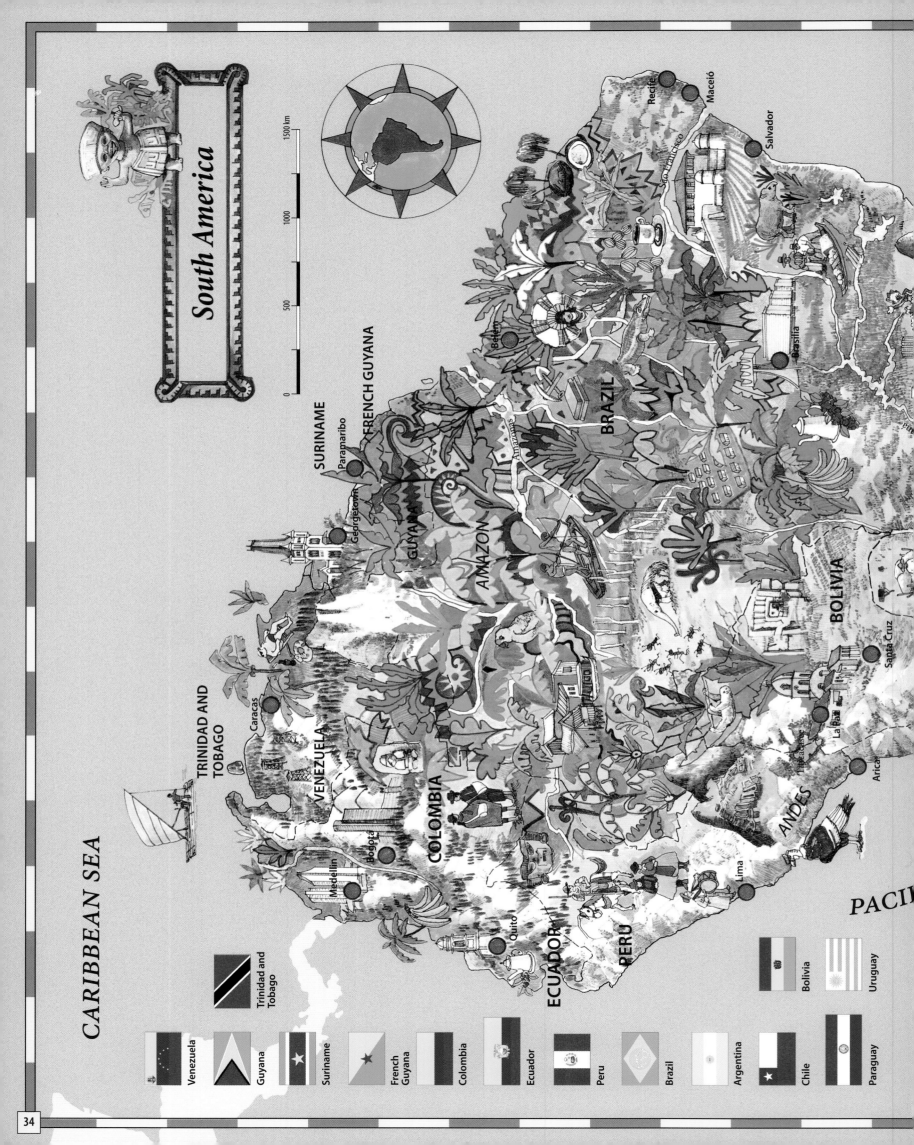

South America

CARIBBEAN SEA

PACIFIC

1500 km
1000
500
0

TRINIDAD AND
TOBAGO

VENEZUELA
Caracas

COLOMBIA
Bogotá
Medellín

ECUADOR
Quito

PERU
Lima

BOLIVIA
Santa Cruz
La Paz
Arica

ANDES

GUYANA
Georgetown

SURINAME
Paramaribo

FRENCH GUYANA

AMAZON
Amazonas

BRAZIL
Belém
Brasília
São Francisco
Recife
Maceió
Salvador

Venezuela
Guyana
Suriname
French Guyana
Colombia
Ecuador
Peru
Brazil
Argentina
Chile
Paraguay

Trinidad and Tobago
Bolivia
Uruguay

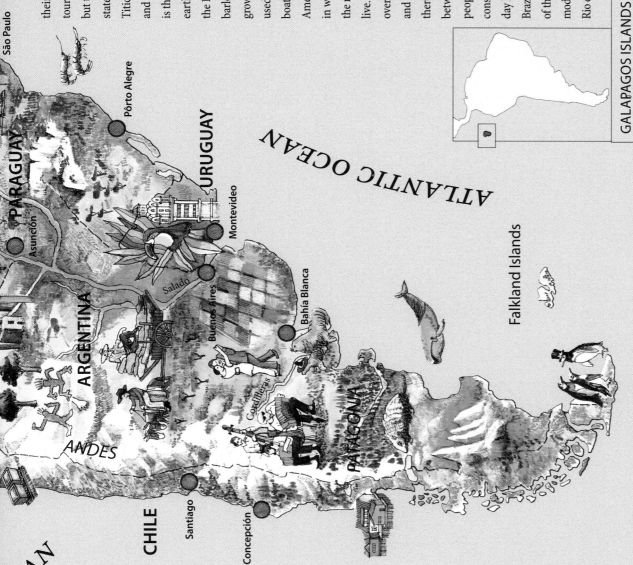

Rio de Janeiro

São Paulo

Pôrto Alegre

PARAGUAY

Asunción

URUGUAY

Montevideo

ARGENTINA

Salado

Buenos Aires

Bahia Blanca

Cordilleras

ANDES

CHILE

Santiago

Concepción

PATAGONIA

ATLANTIC OCEAN

OCEAN

Falkland Islands

GALAPAGOS ISLANDS

San Salvador

Santa Cruz   San Cristóbal

St. Isabela

N o other part of the world comes as close to Antarctica as South America. Ushaia in the province of Tierra del Fuego, Patagonia, is the southernmost city on earth. A cold polar climate reigns here whereas the north of the continent is defined by tropical heat. There are several great rivers in South America that provide plenty of fresh water. Nearly all of them rise in the Cordilleras or Andes mountains which are up to 6000m/19 680 feet high. This mountain range with volcanoes and barren elevated plains spans along the entire western coast of South America, like an insuperable wall. Originally, only Indigenous Native Americans lived in South America. The Incas, masters in manufacturing precious metals, had established a powerful realm in the Andes. But when the Spanish landed in America and began to conquer the land, the Indigenous civilisations perished. The Amazon river carries most water. It springs up in the Andes and crosses the country towards

their pack animal. The air is low in oxygen, and tourists often find they have breathing problems, but the locals aren't affected. La Paz in the Andes state Bolivia is the world's highest capital and Lake Titicaca, located near-by and teeming with fish, is the highest lake on earth. Along its banks, the Indian farmers grow barley and corn. The reeds growing in the water are used for constructing boats. Today, South America is a continent in which many people of the most varied origins live. The metropolises are overly populated; here and in the countryside there is a harsh contrast between excessively rich and very poor people. Luxurious high-rise buildings are constructed close to slums; a large quantity of day labourers work for few big landowners. Brazil and Argentina are the two largest nations of the continent. Brasilia, the capital of Brazil, is a modern city entirely designed on the drawing board. Rio de Janeiro, the former capital, is famous for its

beaches extending for miles on end and for the Carnival parades. The Pampas are the fertile lowlands of Argentina where 50 million cattle are tended by cowboys called gauchos. Its capital, mighty Buenos Aires, is famed as the cradle of Tango music. The most important export goods of South America are bananas, coffee, petroleum, copper, and tin.

Throughout South America, the colonial rulers, mostly Spaniards and Portuguese, constructed buildings in the Baroque style.

the east until it flows into the Atlantic Ocean. It is teeming with piranhas, small fish with extremely sharp teeth that can strip their prey bare to the bone within seconds. The impenetrable jungle of the Amazon region covers 4.5 million square kilometres. Orchids and useful plants such as gummi elasticum grow here, the milky juice of the latter being used to produce rubber.

The jungle is being increasingly deforested to exploit natural resources, produce timber, or lay out new plantations. Scientists fear that this act of deforestation will bring about global changes in climate, affecting the entire planet. The Indio people live in the cold Andes highlands much the same way as hundreds of years ago. They wear colourful, thick woollen ponchos to keep them warm and felt hats to protect them from the sun. The lama, notorious for spitting, is

The mountain tops of the Patagonian Andes in southern South America are covered with snow all year round.

The Galapagos Islands are located to the west of America and belong to Ecuador. They are famous for their unique plant and animal world. The name Galapagos derives from the giant turtles that are indigenous here. These animals can get unusually old, weigh up to 250 kilos and can be 1.5m/ 5 feet long. They are protected animals.

The Arctic

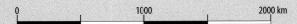

0   1000   2000 km

The northernmost part of the Earth is referred to as the Arctic Regions. The North Pole lies here, in the middle of the ice-covered Arctic Ocean. It wasn't until 1958 that researchers aboard the US-American submarine Nautilus found out that there is no land underneath the ice sheet. The Arctic consists of the ocean plus parts of Canada, Alaska, Siberia, Lapland, and Greenland. The living conditions in the high north are extremely harsh. During the long, dark polar winters, temperatures can sink as low as −40°. In the summer, temperatures only rise to 1–8°C/34–46°F. The Inuit and Sami peoples live from fishing and hunting seals as well as fur-bearing animals such as the arctic fox. The Laplanders are mainly nomadic, roaming the extensive tundra with their reindeer herds. Only few plants thrive in this severe climate and offer food for animals. These are mosses, lichens, grasses, berry shrubs, and dwarf trees. The ice sheet of the Arctic Ocean is several hundred metres thick, in central Greenland it can be up to 3000m/10 000 feet thick. The Arctic Regions are rich in natural resources. An increasing number of people now populates the coastline, where settlements and cities arise – the style of living of the polar people is undergoing a change.

Tobacco pipe of an Inuit, carved out of a walrus dent.

CANADA

Arctic Circle

Baffin
Islands

Nuuk

Huge icebergs drift in the water surrounding Greenland.

This cross section of Greenland shows how the inland is pushed down by masses of ice.

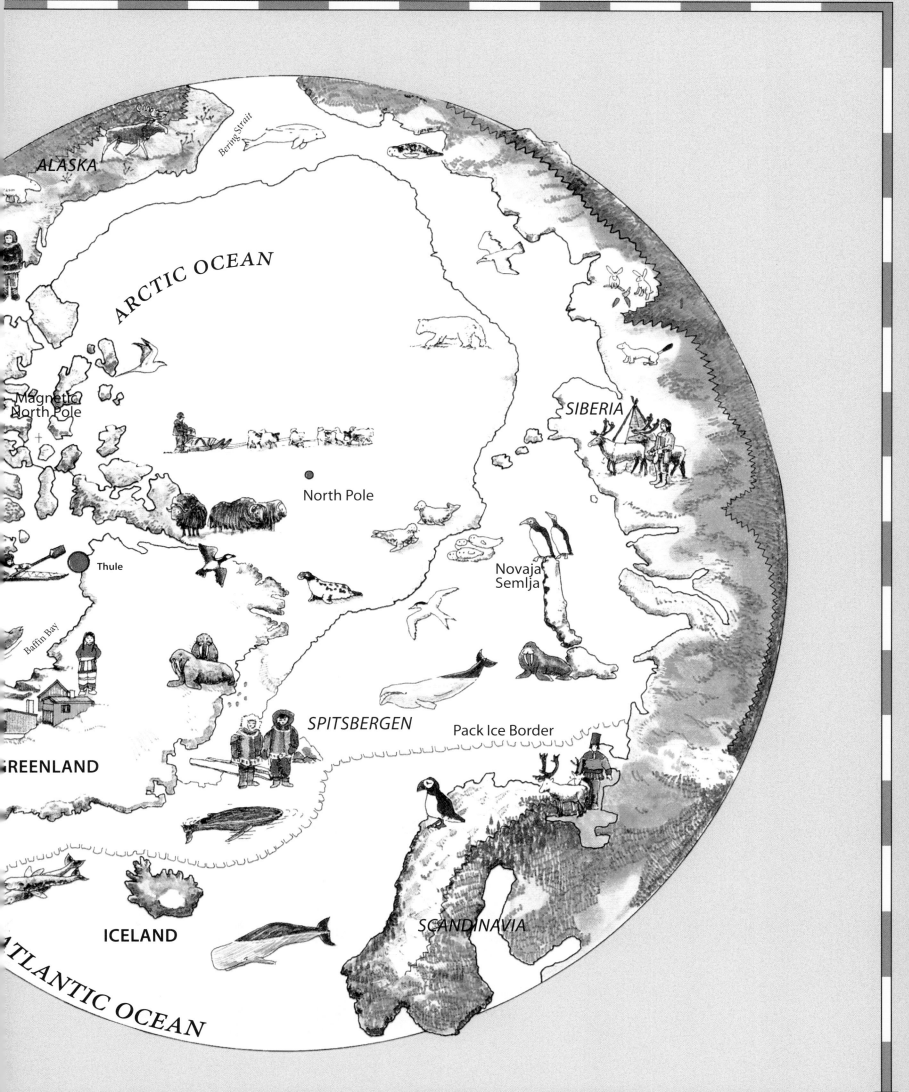

ALASKA

ARCTIC OCEAN

Bering Strait

Magnetic North Pole

North Pole

Thule

Baffin Bay

SIBERIA

Novaja Semlja

SPITSBERGEN

Pack Ice Border

GREENLAND

ICELAND

SCANDINAVIA

ATLANTIC OCEAN

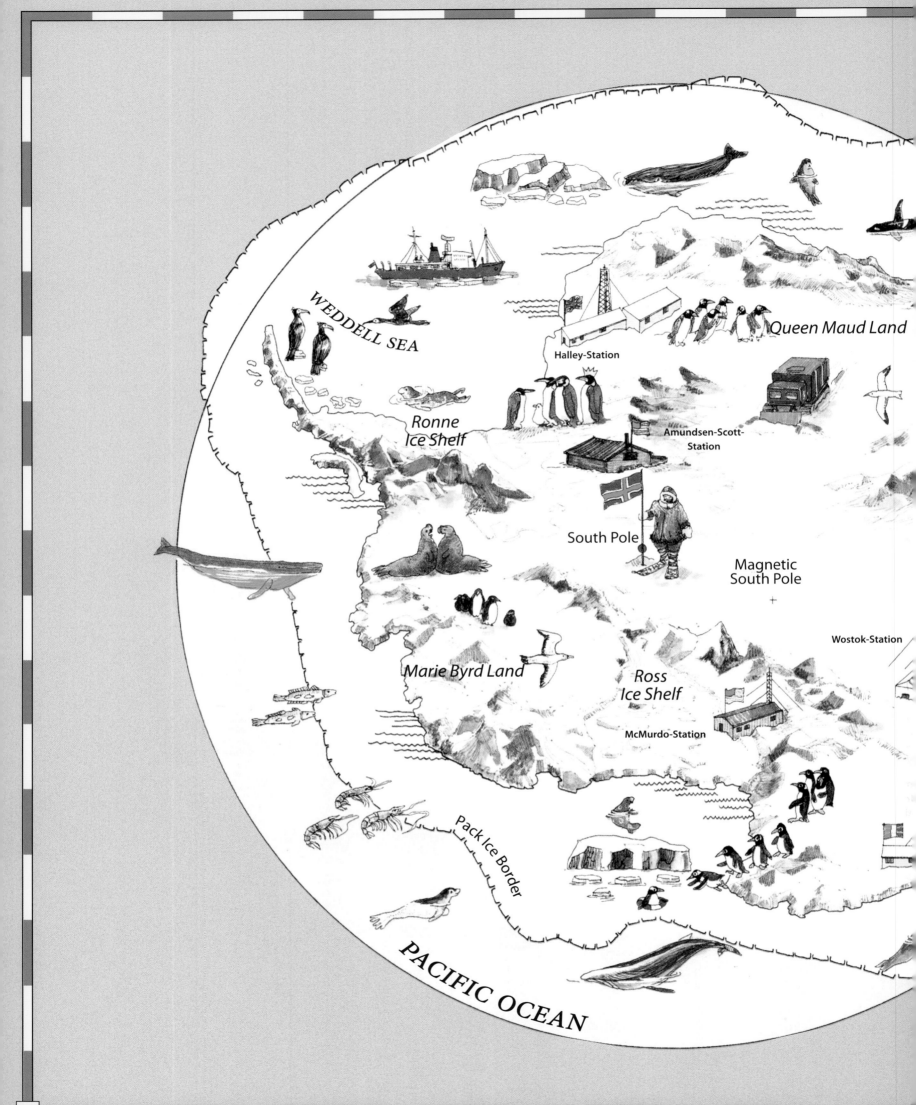

WEDDELL SEA

Queen Maud Land

Halley-Station

Ronne
Ice Shelf

Amundsen-Scott-
Station

South Pole

Magnetic
South Pole

Wostok-Station

Marie Byrd Land

Ross
Ice Shelf

McMurdo-Station

Pack Ice Border

PACIFIC OCEAN

Antarctic Circle

Casey-Base-Station

Wilkes Land

mont
rville-
tion

Antarctica

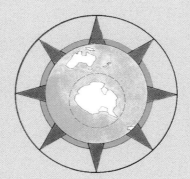

Antarctica is the area surrounding the South Pole. Its land mass is covered by an ice sheet 2000–4000m/6560–13 120 feet thick. Every now and then, gigantic ice blocks break off the glaciers and can endanger passing ships. The climate is extremely harsh. The thermometer can sink as low as –89°C/–128°F; during the warmest month, it is still –30°C/–22°F. Heavy wind gales hit the land, whipping snow and ice across the landscape at an enormous speed. Apart from a limited number of researchers, this area is uninhabited. There are hardly any plants and only few animals manage to survive here. Antarctica is the realm of the penguins, who already feel uncomfortably hot at 0°C/32°F. The Norwegian explorer Roald Amundsen was the first human to reach the South Pole in 1911, beating Englishman Robert Scott by a mere month. Scott and his team died on the long and strenuous way back of famine and cold. So far, it has proved impossible to exploit the natural resources here. Antarctica is an international region and many nations participate in the research projects undertaken here.

Antarctica with its endless ice deserts is the most uninhabitable continent on planet Earth.

Flags of the World

Europe

Albania	Iceland	Austria
Andorra	Italy	Poland
Belgium	Croatia	Portugal
Bosnia-Herzegovina	Latvia	Romania
Bulgaria	Liechtenstein	Russia
Denmark	Lithuania	San Marino
Germany	Luxembourg	Sweden
Estonia	Macedonia	Switzerland
Finland	Malta	Serbia
France	Moldavia	Slovakia
Greece	Monaco	Slovenia
United Kingdom	Montenegro	Spain
Ireland	Netherlands	Czech Republic
	Norway	Turkey

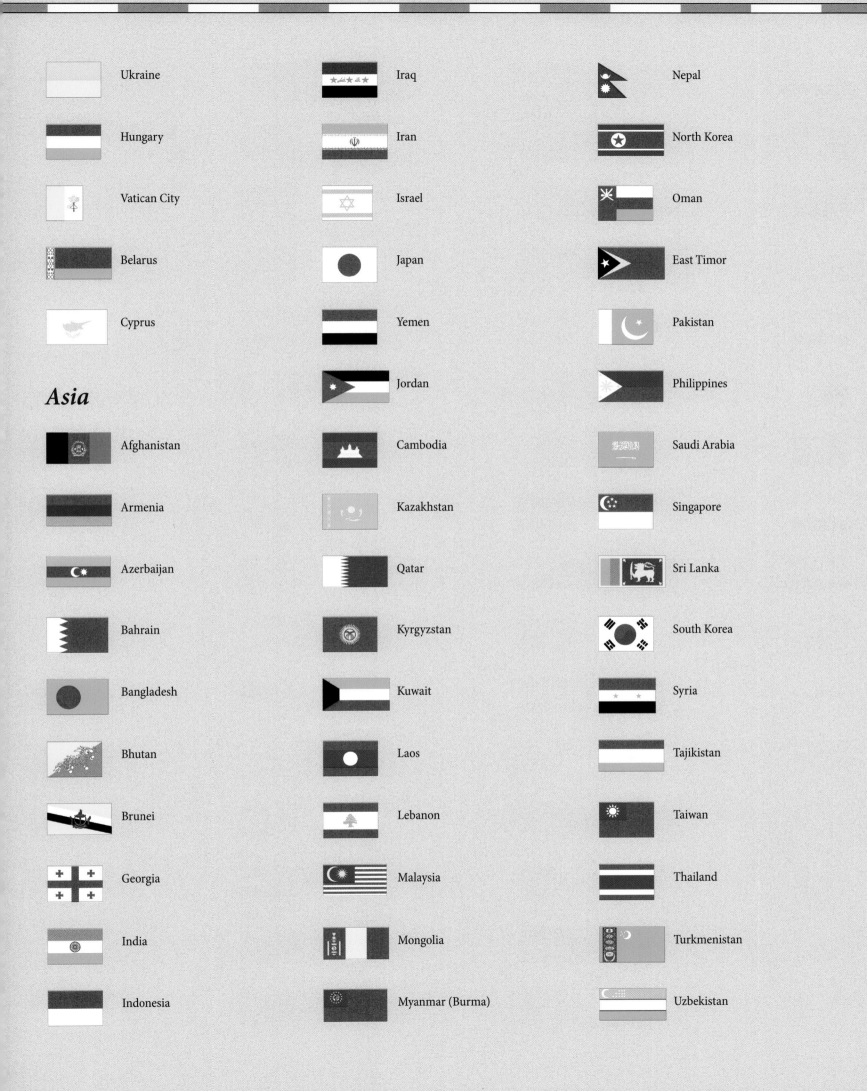

Ukraine

Hungary

Vatican City

Belarus

Cyprus

Asia

Afghanistan

Armenia

Azerbaijan

Bahrain

Bangladesh

Bhutan

Brunei

Georgia

India

Indonesia

Iraq

Iran

Israel

Japan

Yemen

Jordan

Cambodia

Kazakhstan

Qatar

Kyrgyzstan

Kuwait

Laos

Lebanon

Malaysia

Mongolia

Myanmar (Burma)

Nepal

North Korea

Oman

East Timor

Pakistan

Philippines

Saudi Arabia

Singapore

Sri Lanka

South Korea

Syria

Tajikistan

Taiwan

Thailand

Turkmenistan

Uzbekistan

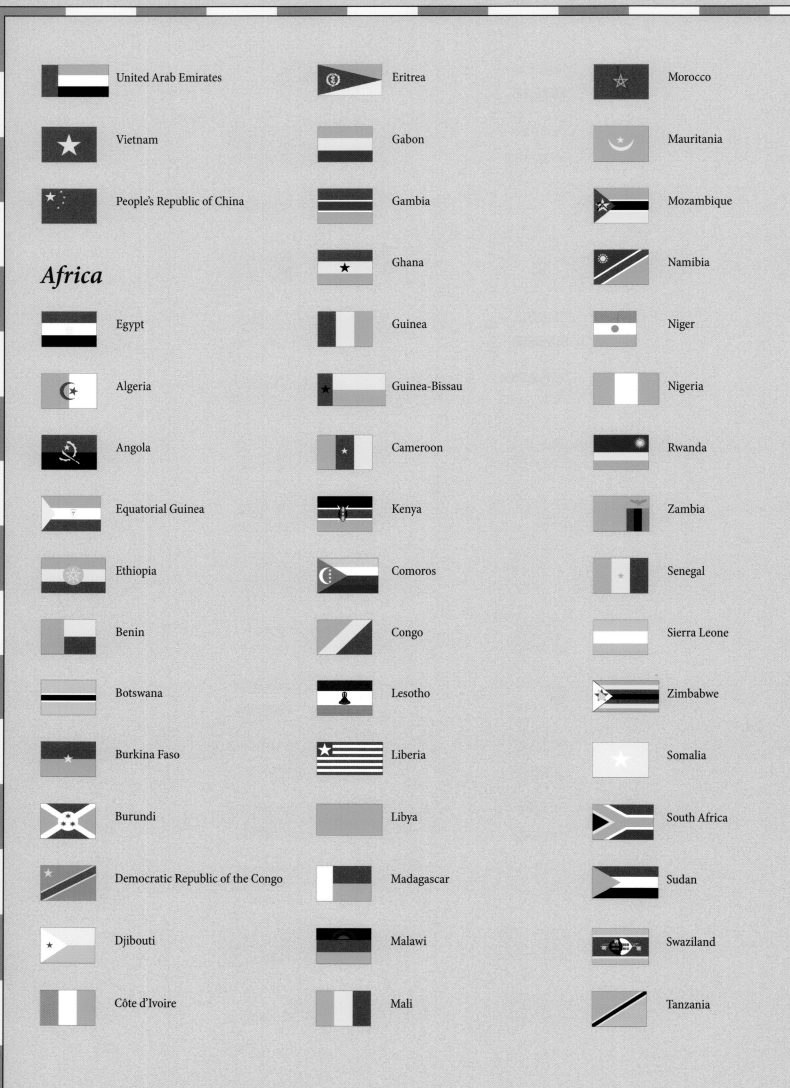

United Arab Emirates

Vietnam

People's Republic of China

Africa

Egypt

Algeria

Angola

Equatorial Guinea

Ethiopia

Benin

Botswana

Burkina Faso

Burundi

Democratic Republic of the Congo

Djibouti

Côte d'Ivoire

Eritrea

Gabon

Gambia

Ghana

Guinea

Guinea-Bissau

Cameroon

Kenya

Comoros

Congo

Lesotho

Liberia

Libya

Madagascar

Malawi

Mali

Morocco

Mauritania

Mozambique

Namibia

Niger

Nigeria

Rwanda

Zambia

Senegal

Sierra Leone

Zimbabwe

Somalia

South Africa

Sudan

Swaziland

Tanzania

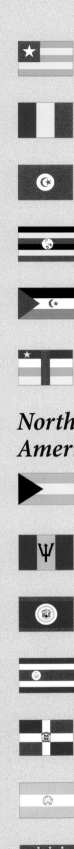

Togo

Chad

Tunisia

Uganda

Western Sahara

Central African Republic

North and Central America

Bahamas

Barbados

Belize

Costa Rica

Dominican Republic

El Salvador

Grenada

Guatemala

Haiti

Honduras

Jamaica

Canada

Cuba

Mexico

Nicaragua

Panama

Puerto Rico

USA

South America

Argentina

Bolivia

Brazil

Chile

Equador

French Guiana

Guyana

Colombia

Paraguay

Peru

Suriname

Trinidad and Tobago

Uruguay

Venezuela

Australia and Oceania

Australia

New Zealand

Papua New Guinea